INCREDIBLE INSECTS

DRAGONFLIES

James E. Gerholdt

Published by Abdo & Daughters, 4940 Viking Drive, Suite 622, Edina, Minnesota 55435.

Copyright © 1996 by Abdo Consulting Group, Inc., Pentagon Tower, P.O. Box 36036, Minneapolis, Minnesota 55435 USA. International copyrights reserved in all countries. No part of this book may be reproduced in any form without written permission from the publisher.

Printed in the United States.

Cover Photo credit: Peter Arnold, Inc.
Interior Photo credits: Peter Arnold, Inc.

Edited by Julie Berg

Library of Congress Cataloging-in-Publication

Gerholdt, James E., 1943
    Dragonflies / by James E. Gerholdt.
    p. cm. — (Incredible insects)
Includes bibliographical references and index.
ISBN 1-56239-484-3
1. Dragonflies—Juvenile literature. [1. Dragonflies.] I. Title. II . Series: Gerholdt, James E., 1943- Incredible insects.
QL520.G47 1995
595.7'33—dc20   95-7391
                                             CIP
                                             AC

Contents

DRAGONFLIES

Dragonflies belong to one of the 28 insect orders. Mayflies and damselflies are in the same order. Insects are arthropods. This means their skeleton is on the outside of their body. They also are ectothermic—they get their body temperature from the environment. There are about 7,000 species in this order, 5,000 of which are dragonflies and damselflies. They are found worldwide.

Dragonflies have four elongated wings, a mouth that can chew, and short antennae. Their bodies are long and slender. They are the most ancient flying insects. Dragonfly fossils date back to the Carboniferous Period, 280 to 350 million years ago!

**Right:
The dragonfly's skeleton is
on the outside of its body.**

LIFE CYCLE

All dragonflies go through a simple metamorphosis. This means they hatch from eggs and spend the first part of their lives as nymphs. The eggs are laid in the water on plants or rocks at water level, or just above it.

The entire nymph stage is spent in the water. Emerald dragonfly nymphs may take five to six years to change into adults. Darter dragonflies take only 30 to 40 days to metamorph. The length of time depends on water temperature and how much food is available to the nymph. Once the nymph sheds its skin, it will spend the rest of its life out of water.

**Right:
A dragonfly larva
feeding on a tadpole.**

SIZES

Dragonflies are large insects. Wingspan determines their size. Wingspan is measured from the tip of one wing to the tip of the other.

Modern dragonflies are not as large as their extinct relatives. Several species from the Carboniferous period had a wingspan of thirty inches (76 cm)! Today's skimmer dragonflies have a one-inch (2.5-cm) wingspan while the darner dragonflies have a three-inch (7.5-cm) wingspan. One tropical species is six inches (15 cm) long. Some nymphs are two inches (5 cm) long.

**Right:
A dragonfly is a large
insect. Its wingspan is
usually twice the length
of its body.**

SHAPES

All dragonflies have similar shapes. They have long, slender bodies and long, narrow wings. The top and bottom wings are shaped the same and are usually unfolded when the dragonfly is not flying. A damselfly folds its wings together when it is not flying. The dragonfly's head and eyes are large.

A nymph has an oddly shaped mouth. The lower lip is folded under the head when it is not being used. When used, it is pushed forward, sometimes as far as one-third of the body length. A pair of lip claws are used to grab prey.

Like all insects, dragonflies have three body parts: the head, thorax, and abdomen. They also have six legs and two antennae.

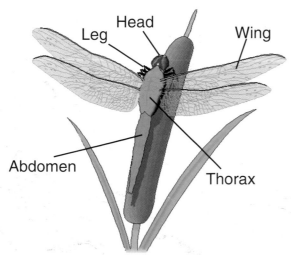

**Right:
The dragonfly's head is
large compared to the
rest of its body.**

COLORS

Some dragonflies are colorful, while others are not. Reds, blues, greens, yellows, browns, and blacks are common colors. In some species, the males have the bright colors and the females have none. Some dragonflies have completely transparent wings with no markings. Other species have blotches on their wings.

The green-eyed skimmer has a brown body with brown blotches on the wings, and bright green eyes. Some darner dragonflies have blue bodies, no markings on their wings, and bright green eyes.

**Right:
Most male dragonfly species are brightly colored; the females are not.**

WHERE THEY LIVE

Adult dragonflies live in many different habitats. They usually stay near the water. But they can also fly long distances.

Some dragonflies sit on plants or rocks near the water, while other species spend most of their time flying. They can even hover like a helicopter! Some species are active during the day, while others prefer the evening. The nymphs always live in water.

**Right:
Adult dragonflies like to
sit on plants near water.**

SENSES

Dragonflies have the same five senses as humans. Their huge eyes can see things a human cannot, and helps them stay active in the evening when there is little light. The nymphs also have good eyesight. But if the water is muddy, they use their antennae to find food.

A male dragonfly may use its wings to lure a female into his territory, either by changing the wingbeat or by flying with one pair of wings at a time. The female can see the changes and hear the wings beating.

**Right:
Close-up of a
dragonfly's eyes.**

**Left:
Close-up of a
dragonfly's head.**

DEFENSE

The dragonfly's best defense is to simply fly away from an enemy. They can fly fast and can change directions quickly.

Some skimmer dragonflies rely on camouflage for defense. Dragonflies will bite if necessary. The bite doesn't hurt, but it can scare humans.

The nymphs use camouflage, and can also bite. While escaping an enemy, they squirt water from their abdomen and swim away.

**Right:
A dragonfly's best
defense is to fly away
from an enemy.**

FOOD

Dragonflies are predators—they eat other animals. The nymphs feed on any insect they can find in the water, using their lower lip (labial mask) to grab prey.

Adult dragonflies hunt in two different ways. Some grab their food in the air while flying. Other species grab prey from plants or the ground. Dragonflies will also gather near a swarm of bees or other insects. Larger species, like the hawker dragonfly, will feed on small frogs. When a dragonfly is flying, it often looks for food.

Right:
A dragonfly feeding
on an insect.

GLOSSARY

Abdomen (AB-do-men) - The rear body part of an arthropod.

Antennae (an-TEN-eye) - A pair of sense organs found on the head of an insect.

Arthropod (ARTH-row-pod) - An animal with its skeleton on the outside of its body.

Camouflage (CAM-uh-flaj) - The ability to blend in with the surroundings.

Carboniferous period (car-bun-IF-er-us) - A period in time 280 to 350 million years ago.

Ectothermic (ek-toe-THERM-ik) - Regulating body temperature from an outside source.

Environment (en-VI-ron-ment) - Surroundings in which an animal lives.

Extinct (ek-STINKT) - A species that has died out.

Fossil (FAH-sill) - The hardened remains or traces of something that lived in a former age.

Habitat (HAB-uh-tat) - An area in which an animal lives.

Insect (IN-sect) - An arthropod with three body parts and six legs.

Labial Mask (LAY-bee-al mask) - The lower lip of a dragonfly nymph that is used to grab food.

Metamorphosis (met-a-MORF-oh-sis) - The change from an egg to an adult.

Nymph (NIMF) - The young of an insect that goes through a simple, or incomplete metamorphosis.

Order (OAR-der) - A grouping of animals.

Predator (PREAD-a-tore) - An animal that eats other animals.

Species (SPEE-seas) - A kind or type.

Thorax (THORE-axe) - The middle body part of an arthropod.

Wingspan - The measurement across the wings from tip to tip.

INDEX

About the Author

Jim Gerholdt has been studying reptiles and amphibians for more than 40 years. He has presented lectures and displays throughout the state of Minnesota for nine years. He is a founding member of the Minnesota Herpetological Society and is active in conservation issues involving reptiles and amphibians in India, Aruba, and Minnesota.

Photo by Tim Judy